SISKIYOU COUNTY LIBRARY

3 2871 004

D0398825

DATE DU

Siskiyou County Library
719 Fourth Street
Yreka, CA 96097

PARROT GENIUS!

And More True Stories of Amazing Animal Talents

By Moira Rose Donohue

NATIONAL GEOGRAPHIC

WASHINGTON, D.C.

Copyright © 2014 National Geographic Society

All rights reserved. Reproduction of the whole or any part of the contents without written permission from the publisher is prohibited.

Published by the National Geographic Society

Gary E. Knell, *President and Chief Executive Officer*
John M. Fahey, *Chairman of the Board*
Declan Moore, *Executive Vice President; President, Publishing and Travel*
Melina Gerosa Bellows, *Publisher and Chief Creative Officer, Books, Kids, and Family*

Prepared by the Book Division

Hector Sierra, *Senior Vice President and General Manager*
Nancy Laties Feresten, *Senior Vice President, Kids Publishing and Media*
Jennifer Emmett, *Vice President, Editorial Director, Kids Books*
Eva Absher-Schantz, *Design Director, Kids Publishing and Media*
Jay Sumner, *Director of Photography, Kids Publishing*
R. Gary Colbert, *Production Director*
Jennifer A. Thornton, *Director of Managing Editorial*

Staff for This Book

Shelby Alinsky, *Project Editor*
Amanda Larsen, *Art Director*
Kelley Miller, *Senior Photo Editor*
Ruth Ann Thompson, *Designer*
Marfé Ferguson Delano, *Editor*
Ariane Szu-Tu, *Editorial Assistant*
Callie Broaddus, *Design Production Assistant*
Grace Hill, *Associate Managing Editor*
Joan Gossett, *Production Editor*
Lewis R. Bassford, *Production Manager*
Susan Borke, *Legal and Business Affairs*

Production Services

Phillip L. Schlosser, *Senior Vice President*
Chris Brown, *Vice President, NG Book Manufacturing*
George Bounelis, *Senior Production Manager*
Nicole Elliott, *Director of Production*
Rachel Faulise, *Manager*
Robert L. Barr, *Manager*

The National Geographic Society is one of the world's largest nonprofit scientific and educational organizations. Founded in 1888 to "increase and diffuse geographic knowledge," the Society's mission is to inspire people to care about the planet. It reaches more than 400 million people worldwide each month through its official journal, *National Geographic,* and other magazines; National Geographic Channel; television documentaries; music; radio; films; books; DVDs; maps; exhibitions; live events; school publishing programs; interactive media; and merchandise. National Geographic has funded more than 10,000 scientific research, conservation, and exploration projects and supports an education program promoting geographic literacy.

For more information, please visit nationalgeographic.com, call 1-800-NGS LINE (647-5463), or write to the following address:

National Geographic Society, 1145 17th Street N.W., Washington, D.C. 20036-4688 U.S.A.

Visit us online at nationalgeographic.com/books

For librarians and teachers: ngchildrensbooks.org

National Geographic supports K–12 educators with ELA Common Core Resources. Visit natgeoed.org/commoncore for more information.

More for kids from National Geographic: kids.nationalgeographic.com

For information about special discounts for bulk purchases, please contact National Geographic Books Special Sales: ngspecsales@ngs.org

For rights or permissions inquiries, please contact National Geographic Books Subsidiary Rights: ngbookrights@ngs.org

Trade paperback
ISBN: 978-1-4263-1770-5
Reinforced library edition
ISBN: 978-1-4263-1771-2

Printed in China
14/RRDS/1

Table of CONTENTS

Einstein is especially curious. That makes her easy to train.

EINSTEIN: PARROT GENIUS!

Einstein joined the Knoxville Zoo in Tennessee when she was five years old.

Chapter 1

IT'S A ZOO HERE!

Imagine you're at the zoo. You hear a tiger growl. That's not surprising. Lots of zoos have tigers. But what if you're nowhere near the tiger exhibit? Next you hear a chimp screech. But there are no chimps around. And then a pirate says, *"Arrgh!"* Is it some kind of trick? Not if you're at the Knoxville (sounds like NOX-vil) Zoo in Knoxville, Tennessee, U.S.A.

Did You Know?

Albert Einstein was a German-born scientist. He was considered a genius and won a Nobel Prize. He also owned a parrot named Bibo.

It means you've just found Einstein, one of the most amazing parrots in the world!

Einstein joined the Knoxville Zoo more than 20 years ago. The zoo wanted to put together an animal show. It hired an animal talent scout. That's someone who looks for awesome animals that can learn to perform. When the talent scout heard about a very smart five-year-old parrot named Einstein, he knew he had to meet her.

Einstein is an African gray parrot. In the wild, African grays live in large groups called flocks. Some flocks have 100 birds. Living in such large groups makes them social, or friendly, with each other.

African gray parrots live in the rain

forests of Africa. But Einstein was not born in Africa. She was hatched in California. Einstein's owners could tell that she was extra smart. That's why they named her after the scientist Albert Einstein. He was so smart that people called him a genius!

The talent scout drove over to meet Einstein. *Would she be as brainy as her namesake?* He hoped so. The breeders introduced him to Einstein. Einstein turned her head this way and that. Then she said a few words to him. That's right—she spoke!

All African gray parrots can mimic sounds. But not all African grays choose to do so. The scout could see that Einstein was naturally chatty. She would be easy to train. He took her to the Knoxville Zoo to try her out for the show.

Parrot Primer

Let's talk parrots:

- There are over 350 types of parrots in the world.
- Parrots usually live in tropical areas. But one type (above), the kea (sounds like KEE-eh), lives in the snowy mountains of southern New Zealand.
- Most parrots are brightly colored. Macaws (sounds like muh-KAWS) are some of the most colorful.
- All parrots have curved beaks.
  - Most parrots eat seeds and fruit. Some eat flowers and bugs.
    - Parrots have four toes on each foot. Two toes point forward and two point backward.
  - The biggest parrots are the macaw (left) and the large cockatoo.

The trainers at the Knoxville Zoo put Einstein in her new home. They knew that like some people, parrots can be afraid of new places. But Einstein wasn't an ordinary parrot. She was curious. She checked out the parrot cage. It was big enough to hold a couple of large dogs. She saw that it had several perches, or branches. It also had three bowls. One was for water. Another was for food—berries and seeds. The third bowl was empty. Soon Einstein would find out what it was for.

In no time, Einstein made herself at home. Zoo trainers put toys in her cage. They gave her shiny beads to play with. They gave her bells to ring. Sometimes they hid food inside tubes. She liked to figure out how to get the food out!

It didn't take the zoo long to decide that Einstein would be good in the show. But she had to be trained. Scientists say that African grays are as smart as five-year-old children. But they behave like two-year-olds. That meant Einstein had a lot to learn.

Teresa Collins became her first head trainer at the zoo. Teresa knew the first thing Einstein needed to learn was to trust her. So she dropped treats into the third bowl in Einstein's cage whenever she walked by. Sometimes she tossed a peanut into the treat bowl. That was the best. Einstein loved peanuts! Einstein soon learned that Teresa made good things happen.

After a while, Teresa tried something new. Instead of dropping a treat into the

bowl, she pinched the food between her
fingers. She held it out to Einstein. African
gray parrots have strong beaks. Teresa
wanted Einstein to take the food gently.
Einstein had learned that Teresa was her
friend. She knew better than to bite the
hand that fed her.

One day, Teresa put
her hand into Einstein's
cage. She hoped Einstein
would climb onto it.
It would mean that
Einstein trusted her.
Trusting a human can
take time, so it's a big step for a parrot.
But not for Einstein. Einstein went to
Teresa right away. She even let Teresa
pet her chest.

Did You Know?

Sometimes African gray
parrots will shrink the
pupils in their eyes,
bob their heads,
stretch their necks, and
throw up. It's a sign
that they love you!

Now Einstein was ready to learn some new words. *How quickly would she learn?* Teresa wondered. We say that African gray parrots "talk." But actually, they mimic, or copy, sounds. They have a lot of muscles (sounds like MUH-sels) in their necks. They use them to change how the air goes through their throats. That makes different sounds. It's kind of like playing a flute.

African grays can make 2,000 different sounds. It's fun for them. But it also protects them. In the wild, some large birds, like hawks, owls, and eagles, feed on parrots. If one grabs an African gray, the bird makes a loud noise. Screech! The large bird lets go of the parrot. Imagine you are about to take a bite of pizza. Suddenly, it screams. You'd drop it pretty fast, too!

Teresa wanted Einstein to copy her. She would speak a word to Einstein. Sometimes Einstein said the word right away. Sometimes Teresa had to repeat it over and over. Teresa discovered that Einstein liked saying lots of words. But sometimes she refused to repeat a word. Parrots will only make sounds they like.

Einstein didn't copy just the sounds her trainers made. She copied *any* sound she liked. She loved the sound of water running. So she taught herself that sound. Once she heard an embarrassing sound. Oops. Someone passed gas. Einstein copied that sound too. Maybe she needs to learn, "Excuse me!"

Parrots can feed themselves with their feet. But this brainy bird can do a whole lot more!

Chapter 2

BIRD BRAIN

One day Teresa had a brainstorm. Einstein lived in a zoo with all kinds of animals. *Would the parrot enjoy making animal sounds?* Teresa wondered. So Teresa howled like a wolf. *"Aaooo!"*

"Aaooo!" Einstein howled back.

"Whoo, whoo, whoooo!" Teresa hooted like an owl.

"Whoo, whoo, whoooo!"

Einstein hooted back. Einstein loved to imitate animal sounds.

After a while, Teresa decided to teach Einstein to make these sounds "on cue." That means making a sound in response to a question. It was harder to teach— and to learn!

First, Teresa waited for Einstein to copy a sound, like "meow." She gave Einstein a treat. Then she asked a question. "What does a cat say?" When Einstein said "meow" again, she got another treat. This time she got a big treat—a peanut! Teresa did this over and over. Soon Einstein said "meow" whenever Teresa asked her what a cat said.

One time Einstein heard a funny sound and started repeating it. It sounded like

"*Arrgh.*" It made her trainer think of a pirate. Pirates often had colorful parrots on their shoulders. So her trainer said, "What do pirates say?"

Did You Know?

Crows are also very intelligent birds. They can make and use tools. One crow was filmed making a wire hook to get food!

"*Arrgh,*" said Einstein. Teresa and Einstein said it over and over. In just a couple of hours, Einstein had a new sound on cue!

Teresa and the other trainers picked out new sounds for Einstein to learn. When they agreed on one, they would all say it to her whenever they saw her. Before long, Einstein could make 200 sounds, including many animal noises! That's more than almost any other parrot, even other African grays.

Einstein stood out because she knew a lot of sounds. And she learned fast. But there are other parrots that can make a lot of sounds. What makes Einstein extra special is that she *remembers* sounds on cue. Most other parrots can only remember 13 or 14 sounds on cue at a time. But that's not how Einstein's brain works. She doesn't forget old cues when she learns new ones. Einstein knows 85 words on cue. She really is amazing!

Does Einstein understand what she's saying? Her trainers say that's a hard question to answer. Sometimes the parrot says something that isn't right. One time, her trainer said, "Make an evil laugh." Usually Einstein says, "*Nyah-ah-ah.*" But this time, Einstein said, "I love you."

But sometimes she says things that make a lot of sense, even if she isn't given a cue. One day a trainer was eating in front of her. "What are you doing?" Einstein asked. She cocked her head. She was looking for a treat. When the trainer didn't give her one, she said, "*Mmmmm,*" like we say when something tastes really good. No one taught her that! Soon she started doing it whenever a trainer was eating. She was training her trainer to give her a treat!

Once Einstein didn't get a treat when she said "*Mmmmm.*" To get her trainer's attention, she lay on her back in her cage. She stuck her feet in the air. She looked right at her trainers. "What are you doing, sweetheart?" she asked. Her trainers thought she was complaining because she wasn't getting a treat. They laughed really hard and gave her one.

Dr. Irene Pepperberg, a scientist, believes that parrots understand language. She wanted to prove her idea. She had a parrot, an African gray parrot named Alex. She trained him and studied him for 30 years. Alex learned over 150 words. And he showed signs of understanding language. So maybe when Einstein seems to understand, she really does!

Even though Einstein knew a lot of words, she had other things to learn before she would be ready for the zoo's show. Her trainers taught her to get in and out of her cage when she was told. And they gave her treats when she stayed on her perch. But she had one more important thing to learn.

Alex, Another Awesome Parrot

Scientists have taught apes to understand human language. Dr. Pepperberg tried to do the same thing with her parrot, Alex. She showed him different colored things. Then she asked him to pick out something blue. He did, over and over. She asked him how many items he saw. He would count up to six things. Sometimes Alex asked for something. If Dr. Pepperberg gave him the wrong item, he told her. She thought this showed that he could understand.

Did You Know?

Most birds use their beaks to pick up food. Parrots are the only birds that can lift food into their mouths with their feet. Not many people can do that!

In the show, called *Animals in Action,* Einstein would help teach visitors about parrots in the wild. She would also show them how birds are trained. But she would have to talk into a microphone so the audience could hear her.

Some parrots get shy about talking into a microphone. They move away. They stop talking. Teresa wondered how Einstein would react to the microphone.

"Here, Einstein," Teresa said. "Let's practice." She held up the microphone. It was the first time Einstein had seen one. But the chatty parrot wasn't nervous at all. She leaned in. She said all her words on cue. She was ready for the show!

The day of her first show soon arrived. The audience filed into the outdoor theater and took their seats. Einstein looked at them. Teresa asked her a question. She held up the microphone. Einstein answered. She asked another question. Einstein answered that too. She remembered everything. She really was a parrot genius!

The audience couldn't believe it. They clapped and clapped. They told their friends about Einstein. Soon everyone in Knoxville was talking about the brilliant parrot.

Shy away from a microphone? Not Einstein. This bird's a superstar!

Chapter 3

SUPERSTAR!

The people at a local TV show heard about Einstein. They invited her to be on the show. Soon she was invited to be on other radio and TV shows.

Then Einstein got her big break. She was invited to an animal talent show! By then Einstein had a new trainer—Stephanie White. She and Stephanie were going to be on national TV. It was a great chance for people to see what Einstein could do. And Stephanie wasn't worried. She knew Einstein was a natural performer.

Stephanie and Einstein flew to California, U.S.A. They waited backstage at the TV studio. Other animals performed. Then the announcer introduced Einstein. Stephanie and Einstein took the stage. Stephanie stood in front of a sparkly blue curtain covered with stars. She wore a green shirt and pants with pockets. That's where she kept treats for Einstein.

Einstein stood on a perch. She looked out at the bright lights. And the cameras. And the big audience. She had seen that all before. But there was something more this time. Three judges sat in front of the stage. This was more than just a TV show. It was also a talent *contest*.

Stephanie smiled at the audience. Then she held the microphone up to Einstein. "Are you excited?" she asked the bird.

"*Whoooo!*" said Einstein. Then Stephanie asked the parrot her name. Einstein made a funny sound. "*Unnh, unnh, unnh.*" It didn't sound like "Einstein." Uh-oh.

Stephanie frowned. Was Einstein suddenly camera shy? How embarrassing if Einstein didn't want to perform! Then she figured it out. "She's just clearing her throat," she said. Stephanie tried again. She asked Einstein to say her name.

"Einstein," she said. Nice and loud. And then she said, "Hi, sweetheart." Stephanie knew then that everything would be all right.

Protect the Parrots!

Wild African gray parrots live in Africa. But they are popular pets in other countries. So people in Africa catch them. They ship them around the world. But they're not always careful. Sometimes they wipe out entire flocks. Sometimes they don't care for the birds that are shipped. The birds die. Some countries try to protect parrots. Now people need permission to bring them into the United States. If you want a parrot for a pet, consider buying one from a local breeder.

She asked Einstein to make some animal sounds. Einstein howled like a wolf. Then she growled like a tiger. She mimicked a chimp and a pig. Then Stephanie said, "How about a skunk?"

Einstein said, "Stinker."

Then Stephanie told Einstein to make sound effects. Einstein made the sound of water going down a drain. Then she made a spaceship noise. She did her evil laugh. *Nyah-ah-ah.* The judges laughed. So did the audience. Einstein bobbed a little dance with Stephanie. She fluffed up her feathers.

Then Stephanie said she had a problem. "What's the matter?" asked Einstein. Stephanie told Einstein she had lost her dog. Einstein whistled. "Come here!" she said.

At the end of the show, Stephanie asked, "Are you famous?"

Einstein put her beak right up to the microphone. "Superstar!" she whispered. One judge's mouth fell open.

But Einstein was right. She was a superstar! And she won the talent contest! Now she really was famous. More TV shows invited her to appear. She was on *Good Morning, America,* the *Early Show,* and the *Late Show.* She was even on the *Tonight Show.* The host was impressed. He had had birds on his show before. But Einstein was the only bird that did what she was supposed to do!

In 2008 Stephanie left the zoo. She became a teacher. Einstein got a new head trainer. Her name was Nikki Edwards.

Nikki grew up on a farm near Knoxville. Her father owned a pet store. She's always lived around animals. When she was little, she used to sit outdoors and stretch her arms out. She waited for birds to land on them. When she got older, Nikki wanted to work with animals. So she joined the circus. She was even in a circus act.

After a while, Nikki came home. She started working at the Knoxville Zoo. Now Nikki travels with Einstein to her appearances. They've toured all around the country. When they fly, Einstein travels in a small cage that fits under the seat.

One time there was a problem with their plane. It sat on the runway for several hours. People got nervous. Then a strange beeping sound started. Now the people on the plane were really worried. But Nikki wasn't. She bent down. She looked under the seat. "Be quiet, Einstein," she whispered. It wasn't the right time to make a noise like that!

Einstein sometimes makes mistakes when she performs. She might say, "No," when she is supposed to say, "Yes." When that happens, her trainers try to change the conversation. Sometimes it works. Sometimes they just have to laugh.

Laughing is actually Einstein's favorite sound to mimic. She does her evil laugh. And she does a great Santa Claus laugh. "Ho-ho-ho," she says in a deep voice. Sometimes she makes laughing sounds for

Did You Know?

The most common species of bird in the world is ... the chicken! Chickens can make over 30 sounds to warn about different dangers.

fun. That gets the trainers laughing. And then Einstein laughs even more!

In 2014, Einstein turned 27 years old. Einstein is very busy. She is now the star of the zoo. She and Nikki perform three shows a day during the summer. During the school year, they visit schools. They also visit local community centers. At their shows, Einstein and Nikki teach people about wild African grays. They show people what African gray parrots can do. And they teach everyone about being good pet owners.

Someday you might visit the Knoxville Zoo. You might hear a certain animal sound when there's no sign of that animal. But now you'll know what it is. It's the sound of a superstar!

Will and Otis soar above the clouds. Otis is as happy as a dog with his head out a car window.

OTIS:
WHEN
PUGS FLY

Otis looked at Will with big puppy eyes like this pug. Will knew this was the dog for him.

Chapter 1

PUG or PIG?

One hot summer day in 2001, Will da Silva left his home near Sacramento, California. He drove to a house a few miles away. He was a little nervous. He wasn't sure what he would find there. But he was also excited. He was hoping to meet someone he would fall in love with.

Will knocked and a woman came to the door. "I've come about

Did You Know?

Adult pugs stand 12 to
14 inches (30 to 35 cm) tall.
On average, they weigh
between 14 and 18 pounds
(6 and 8 kg).

your ad," Will said.

"Come on in,"
said the woman.

When Will stepped
through the door, eight pairs of big, brown
eyes looked at him. They belonged to eight
pug puppies. They all had wrinkled,
"pushed-in" faces. They looked as if they
had walked into a door without opening it
first! Pugs sometimes come in black, but
these were all tan colored, with black faces
and ears. Will had come to buy one of the
puppies from the woman and her husband.
Their pug was the mother of this litter
of puppies.

The eight little pugs cocked their heads
up at Will. It seemed like they were trying
to figure him out. Then one puppy ran up

to him. Will tickled his belly. The puppy
licked Will's nose. When Will put him
down, the pup pawed at Will's leg. He
ran around in circles in front of Will.
He wagged his curly little tail.

Will tried to play with the other
puppies, but the first one wouldn't let him.
He nudged the others away. He climbed
over Will's feet. *Don't play with the others,*
he seemed to say. *Pick me!*

The other puppies ran and barked and
wrestled with one another. But not that
first puppy. He followed Will around.
He wouldn't leave him alone.

Will sat down and looked into the
puppy's big eyes. Will had wanted a pug
ever since he was a kid and saw a movie
called *The Adventures of Milo and Otis.*

What's in a Name?

It's easy to see why some people might confuse pugs and pigs. Their names sound similar. They both have curly tails. They both snort. Some pigs are kept as family pets. But pugs are dogs, of course. The first pug dogs probably came from China. We don't know for sure how they got their name. It may have come from the Latin word *pugnus*, which means "fist." The word "pug" is also an old nickname for a monkey. And some monkeys have "pushed-in" faces— just like pugs!

The movie is about two best friends—a cat named Milo and a pug named Otis. The friends get separated. But they never give up looking for each other. Something about that pug's loyalty made Will want a pug of his own. And this puppy seemed loyal to Will already. *This was the puppy for him,* Will decided. He already knew what to name him. Otis, of course!

"Come on, Otis. Let's go home," Will said. He paid for the puppy and put him into the cardboard box he had brought. Off they went. Poor Otis cried and whined the whole ride. He wanted to get out of the box and run around.

When they got home, Will carried the box into his house. Otis hopped right out. He ran here and there, like he was looking for something. Then he ran in circles. *What in the world?* It was like the puppy wanted something. *Aha! Maybe Otis is hungry,* Will thought. He gave him a bowl of puppy chow. Otis gobbled it up. Then the pup wanted dessert. He found it— Will's sandal! *Mmmmm*. It became his favorite toy.

After Otis finished eating, Will decided it was time to introduce the puppy to his other dog, Rocky. Rocky was big and strong. He was a Rottweiler (sounds like ROT-wy-ler). Rottweilers were bred to work as guard dogs or herding dogs. But they are also family pets, like Rocky. Rocky was black with tan on his face and paws. His coloring was the opposite of Otis's.

Will carried Otis over to Rocky. Otis hung back. His curly tail uncurled. The puppy seemed a little bit afraid. After all, Rocky's head alone was bigger than all of Otis!

Then Otis noticed the couch. It was long way up for a little puppy. He backed up, crouched down, and sprang! He made it. Then he climbed even higher, all the way to the top. "He found his spot on the top of the couch cushion," Will said. It would soon become his favorite spot to sit or to nap.

Of course, Rocky jumped onto the couch too. Otis's wrinkled face looked nervous. But he didn't need to be worried. Rocky sniffed Otis with his big nose. Then he snuggled up right next to Otis.

In no time, Rocky became like a big brother to him. He played with Otis. He even licked Otis's ears to clean them out.

Otis loved Will's daughter, Nicole, from the start. Nicole liked to put on shows and dress up in costumes. One day she might be a princess. Another day, Nicole was a rock star. Sometimes she needed another actor for her plays. "Otis, you be the clown," she would say. Then she dressed him up too. Otis didn't mind. He sat there quietly, cocking his head and looking cute.

Otis adored Will and Rocky and Nicole. But more than anything, he loved

Did You Know?

Dog breeds are divided into seven groups: sporting, nonsporting, hound, terrier, toy, working and herding. Pugs are in the toy group.

food. Especially bacon. When he wanted a snack, he ran in circles. *Give me treats,* he seemed to say. He even stole Rocky's food when Rocky wasn't looking. But Rocky didn't do anything. He just let Otis have his food. Will called Otis an "eat-aholic."

Sometimes Otis ate strange things—things that weren't food at all. One day Nicole opened her crayon box and found that some colors were gone. "Dad! Crayons are missing again," she reported. They both knew what had happened. Otis had stolen them. But he couldn't help himself. To him they were "pug-a-licious." He couldn't hide his crime, either. After Otis ate crayons, his poop came out rainbow colored. Otis the pug loved to pig out!

Otis shows off the special harness created for him by parachute maker Pete Swan.

High-Flying PUG

Otis always looked sad when Will left for work. And Will hated leaving the puppy at home. One day he had his hand on the doorknob and was about to leave when he thought, *I wonder if Otis would like to come with me.*

"Hey, Otis," he called. "Want to go to work with me?" The pug perked up. "OK, let's go then!"

Will said. Otis hopped into the car with him and off they went.

Will taught skydiving at Lodi (sounds like LOW-die) Airport in Acampo, California. When he and Otis got there, the pug made friends with the other skydivers, or jumpers, right away. He did his little circle dance for them. It made them laugh. Some of the jumpers gave Otis treats. Of course, Otis loved that!

Whenever Will went up in a plane with a student, Otis explored the parachute center at the airport. One day, he spied another dog. It was a schnauzer named Jessie. Jessie belonged to the owner of the "drop zone." That's the field where the jumpers land. Otis waited for Will there. Will said that over the years it became "Otis's favorite place to be."

Otis and Jessie loved to hang out together. Sometimes they got into a little trouble. While they were waiting for the skydivers, they got hungry. They sniffed around the backpacks at the drop zone and found the jumpers' lunches. Sometimes Otis helped himself to a sandwich—or two.

Otis became "a regular" out at the airport—just like Will. Skydiving wasn't just Will's job. It was what he loved. His first skydive was right after high school to celebrate his graduation. New skydivers don't jump alone. They are strapped to the front of an experienced skydiver. They share a parachute. This is called a "tandem" jump. Will loved skydiving right away. He wanted to jump by himself.

He's been skydiving ever since that first time. He has made over 13,000 jumps!

Will knew that dogs skydive for the military. They jump into hard-to-reach areas to spy on the enemy or sniff for bombs. That gave Will an idea.

"I'm thinking about taking Otis for a jump," he said to his skydiving pals one day. "What do you think?"

"Sure, go for it," they said.

"What do you think, Otis?" Will asked. Otis wagged his curly tail. "OK," said Will. "I think that means yes!"

The military uses big dogs, like German shepherds. They are strapped to the soldier across the soldier's chest, forming a *t*. But Otis was small. Will thought the pug could be strapped to his chest upright, like

Did You Know?

**A person
who makes parachutes
is called a rigger.**

a kangaroo in its
mother's pouch. It
would be like a beginner's tandem jump.
It would feel like true skydiving.

But first Otis needed the right
equipment. Will took Otis to meet a
master parachute maker named Pete Swan.
"Do you think you could make a special
harness for Otis?" Will asked.

"Sure," Pete said. Pete designed a
harness that strapped Otis to Will's chest,
with his head under Will's chin. The pup's
front paws were free. He and Will would
use the same parachute for the jump. Will
just hoped Otis wouldn't try to eat the
parachute first!

Otis also needed something to protect
his eyes from the wind. So Will took him to

the pet store. Will bought Otis a special pair of doggy goggles. Doggy goggles let dogs do other sports too, such as waterskiing.

Will waited until Otis was around a year old to take him on his first jump. It would be a "hop-and-pop." That's a jump from a low height—only 3,000 feet (914 m). Low? That's like jumping off a very tall skyscraper! But it's low for a skydiver. Ten seconds after jumping, Will would open, or pop, the parachute. Then they would float for three to five minutes.

Will picked a bright, sunny day. He put on his own harness. He attached Otis's new harness to his front. He slipped the pup in. Then Will slid the goggles on Otis. Otis looked pretty cool. They would strap on their parachute in the plane.

Jumping for the Military

During World War II, dogs helped the army. Some of them were trained as messengers. Some carried supplies. But some jumped out of planes. They were called "parapups." These dogs parachuted into hard-to-reach areas. Sometimes they were strapped to their handlers. Sometimes they jumped by themselves. The dogs helped track down lost soldiers whose planes crashed in snowy, icy areas near the North Pole. Then they pulled them on sleds to safety. Soldiers say that the dogs wagged their tails the whole time!

In no time, the plane reached the height for their jump. Will and Otis stood at the open door of the plane. *Whoosh!* The air rushed past them. Otis looked around nervously. He squirmed in his harness. *I don't know about this,* he seemed to be thinking. But Will knew that all first-time skydivers are a little scared. He took a deep breath and jumped.

The minute they left the plane, Otis's tongue came out. His ears blew back. He looked around at the scenery. He was like a dog "sticking his head out of the car window," says Will. When

Did You Know?

The first record of a dog skydiving was in 1785. A French balloonist dropped his dog several hundred feet over the side of his balloon.

they landed, Otis jumped out of his harness and ran around in circles. He wanted a treat, of course!

Not long after their first jump, Will decided to take Otis on another one. He wondered if the pug would be afraid to get into his harness this time. But Otis climbed right in. This time they did a full jump—from 13,000 feet (3,962 m) in the air! That was more than four times higher than Otis's first jump.

Soon Otis was hooked on skydiving, just like Will. As soon as Will brought out his harness, Otis hopped in. Sometimes Otis got *too* excited. Will says, "The hardest part was teaching Otis not to jump into the airplane without his gear on!"

Will and Otis, in his rock-star doggy goggles, share their favorite sport—skydiving!

Otis couldn't get enough of skydiving. But Will had work to do. He taught new students how to skydive. He filmed other jumpers. Sometimes he even flew the plane. He couldn't take Otis with him every time.

One day, Will was going on a jump without Otis. Otis pawed at him. *Please take me,* the pug seemed to beg. "Not this time, Otis," Will told the pup. As the plane started down the runway, Will looked out the window. He couldn't believe his eyes. Otis was chasing the plane! He didn't want to be left behind—he wanted to jump!

Will saw how much Otis liked meeting other jumpers and how much they liked meeting Otis. "Otis," he said to the pug, "let's have a boogie." A boogie isn't a dance. It's a skydivers' party. It usually takes place at the drop zone. Skydivers chat, make friends, and eat snacks. Did someone say snacks? Otis was in!

Otis and Will hosted an "Otis Boogie" at Lodi Airport. Skydivers from all over the area came to meet Otis. They were amazed by the skydiving pug. Pretty soon, more and more people were talking about

Otis. Jumpers started coming from around the world. They called him "king of the drop zone." Otis was famous!

Before long, some jumpers asked Will, "Can I jump with Otis?" Will was always very careful when he took Otis on jumps. He wasn't going to let just anyone skydive with his beloved pug. He only said "yes" to people he trusted. One of those people was a wingsuit jumper named Ed Pawlowski.

Wingsuiting is skydiving in a special kind of suit. The suit is puffy. It has cloth between the legs and cloth between the arms and the body. If you saw one, you might think of a bat. Or a flying squirrel! The wingsuit slows the fall. The jumper opens the parachute only at the very end. Ed would strap Otis to his wingsuit.

Will has never been wingsuiting. He watched Otis proudly from the ground. As far as Will knew, Otis was the only dog to ever do a wingsuit dive.

Otis loved all the attention. But fame didn't change him— he still loved food best of all! Wherever there was food and no one looking, Otis was there. He tiptoed by. Poof! Another lunch disappeared!

Did You Know?

Every dog's nose print is different. Just like human fingerprints, a nose print can be used to identify a dog.

Then one day Will had a problem with Otis's harness. It didn't fit. He couldn't fasten the straps! Uh-oh. Otis had gobbled down too many treats. He'd stolen too many lunches. The piggy little pug's lifestyle had caught up with him!

Will took Otis to the vet. The vet said the pudgy dog had to lose some weight. That meant no more treats! Will wanted Otis to keep skydiving with him. Most of all, Will wanted to keep Otis healthy. So he put Otis on a diet.

Otis was hungry. He missed his treats. He would dance around by the pantry and beg at the drop zone. But Will and the other jumpers said, "No." Being on a diet was tough. But it was worth it. Little by little, Otis slimmed down.

"OK, boy. Let's see if you can slip into your harness now," Will told his dog. It fit. Hooray! Now Will could take Otis skydiving again.

In 2010, Will and Otis entered a skydiving contest called the Best of the

West. It takes place at Lodi every year. Ten skydivers jump out of a plane. They join hands in the sky to build a circle as fast as they can. That's called a ten-way speed star jump. The fastest group to make the speed star wins. Otis was the only dog in the contest. His group won. He even got a certificate!

Then Otis got a big surprise. One day in August 2011, a news team showed up at Lodi Airport. They had cameras. They had microphones. They had a reporter. It was the local TV show, *Good Day Sacramento*. They were there to film Otis skydiving. He was going to be a TV star!

The weather was hot, but the sky was clear. Planes took off. Skydivers jumped. Colorful parachutes appeared in the blue sky.

Summertime Dog Care

Dogs sweat through their paws. They also pant to cool themselves down. It's harder for pugs to cool down because they have such short snouts. They need special care in hot weather. But all dogs need to be watched carefully in the summer. Here are some hot weather tips:

- Never leave a dog alone in a car with the windows up, even for a minute.
- Walk dogs on grass instead of hot cement sidewalks or streets.
- Always have plenty of water for dogs to drink.

They looked like mini rainbows. The reporter watched from the drop zone as jumper after jumper landed.

"Is that him?" the reporter asked. Will's daughter, Nicole, was there that day. She shook her head "no." Then she pointed to a blue-striped parachute.

"That's my dad," she said. And Otis, of course. Pretty soon Will and Otis landed on the ground—a perfect landing.

"Otis was on the top of his A-game that day," said Will. He meant Otis had done his best.

When they reached the ground, Otis leaped out of his harness. He shook himself. He ran around in circles. Then he sat down in front of the camera looking like, well, the star that he was!

Otis's jump was shown on TV. He became more famous than ever. But Otis was getting older. He got tired more easily. Will decided that it was time for the skydiving pug to retire. Otis didn't seem to mind. As long as he could still hang out with Will and Nicole—and get treats!—he was happy.

Someday Will may get another dog. But he doesn't plan to take it skydiving. That was just for Otis. Otis was his "once in a lifetime dog."

Mudslinger shows off his Frisbee skills while an audience looks on.

MUDSLINGER: HAMMING IT UP!

At bedtime, Mudslinger loves to wedge himself between the other pigs.

PIGS in a BLANKET

O ne winter day in 2007, John Vincent hung up the phone and turned to his wife, Debbie. "He sounds perfect," he told her. "They're flying him out tomorrow."

John wasn't talking about a person. The passenger he would be meeting at the airport in Denver, Colorado, was a six-month-old potbellied pig.

John had been on the phone with someone from the Pig Placement Network in New York City. It's a rescue group that finds new homes for unwanted pigs. This pig's former owners lived in an apartment. They found out that they couldn't keep a pig there. So they put it up for adoption.

John had seen a picture of the young pig on the Internet. He called to find out more about it. He learned that the pig was very outgoing. The rescue group worker told John that they sometimes took the pig to visit sick people in hospitals. The pig had to ride on elevators, which can be scary for a lot of animals. But this little pig just walked right on.

"That told me he was confident," John said. "I knew I wanted him."

The next day, John drove to the airport in Denver to meet the pig. It was in a pet travel crate. John knew that even the most confident animal can get nervous on an airplane. So he did everything he could to keep the pig relaxed. He slowly wheeled the crate right up to his van. He slid open the van door. Then he opened the crate door. The young pig walked right into the van, as if he knew he belonged there!

John and the pig took a long look at each other. The pig was very cute. He was all pink, with tiny black markings on his face. Like other potbellied pigs, he had a straight tail and small ears.

Then the pig surprised John. He flopped down and rolled onto his side. That meant he was comfortable with John already. It also meant he wanted his belly scratched. John rubbed his tummy.

He knew this little piggy was a keeper. "Come on, little fellow," he said. "We're going home." John named the pig Mudslinger.

John lived on a ranch in Franktown, Colorado. He had always loved animals. He had owned dogs for ages. Then about 20 years ago, some friends told him to think about getting a pet pig. *A pig?* John wasn't sure. But he went to take a look at some potbellied piglets.

The piglets squirmed. They squealed. And they snuffled their flat little snouts, or noses, over everything. Pigs, which are also known as hogs, use their snouts to dig in the ground. That's how they find food.

Potbellied Profile

Potbellied pigs are originally from Vietnam. They usually weigh between 80 and 160 pounds (36 and 73 kg). That's smaller than most American or European farm pigs. Like all pigs, potbellies have no sweat glands. So they wallow in mud or water to stay cool. They mostly eat grains, veggies, and sometimes fruit. Though they can be shy at first, potbellied pigs are social animals. They bond easily with humans and are known to especially love belly rubs!

Did You Know?

Wild pigs existed as far back as six million years ago. They are related to the hippopotamus!

John fell in love with the wiggly piggies. He brought one home and named him Bacon.

John and Bacon got along so well that John decided to get another potbellied pig. Over the years, John's pig family grew. By the time John brought Mudslinger home, Bacon had passed away, but there were four other potbellied pigs at the ranch. Their names were Pork Chop, Hoover, Peewee, and Zorro. These pigs lived inside John's house, with him and his wife, Debbie. That's where Mudslinger would live, too.

Before John introduced Mudslinger to the other potbellied pigs, he wanted him to feel comfortable in the house. He took him into the living room. Many pigs are fearful in new places. But not Mudslinger. He pranced right in. He looked around. Then he looked at John. John said he could almost hear Mudslinger say, *This will do.*

Now it was time to meet the family. John let the other pigs into the living room. He watched them all closely. Certain pigs are bosses. Sometimes a boss pig can push a little one into a corner and hurt it. Young pigs usually stay away from the big boss hogs.

Mudslinger amazed him again. "Mudslinger was friendly," John said. "He didn't start any fights. He fit right in." The other pigs seemed to like Mudslinger right away. In no time, he became part of John's potbellied pig family.

Even though the potbellies lived in John's house, they didn't eat in the dining room with him and his wife. John had built the pigs their own room for mealtimes. Pigs are clean animals, but they are messy eaters. And they like to eat a lot. At feeding time, Pork Chop, Hoover, Peewee, and Zorro could be, well, piggy. They had poor manners. Some of them would shove the others away from their bowls. They hogged the food. But not Mudslinger. He was a little gentleman right from the start.

The potbellies also had their own bedroom inside the house. It was piled high with blankets. When it was cold, the pigs snuggled into the blankets and covered themselves up. All you could see were their snouts sticking out.

At bedtime, Mudslinger climbed right into the pile of pigs and blankets. He wasn't shy. He didn't sleep at the end of the row. No, that poised (sounds like POYZD) little pig walked across the backs of the bigger pigs. He squirmed and wormed and wiggled his way in. Soon he was wedged between two pigs. Then he nodded off to sleep. John smiled. He nicknamed Mudslinger the "wedge" hog.

Did You Know?

Pigs weigh about 2.5 pounds (1.1 kg) at birth. Some kinds grow up to weigh 700 pounds (300 kg) or more.

Mudslinger uses his super-sensitive snout to check the mail.

PIGHEADED

John was not only a pig lover; he was also a pig trainer. It all started when he got his first pig, Bacon. "I thought people were going to make fun of me for having a pet pig," John said. "So I started training him because I wanted my pig to be better than their dogs."

John trained Bacon like he would train a dog. He praised him.

He gave him dog biscuits. It worked. "It seemed like Bacon learned faster than my dogs did," said John.

Soon John became interested in animal training. He read books about it. He went to a class. Then he took classes with experts. Before long, John was an expert, too.

Maybe I should put together a little show, John thought. It would be fun. And people could see how clever his pigs were. He decided to call his troupe (sounds like TROOP) of little hams "Top Hogs." The show became a hit. Soon, John and his potbellies were performing all over the country.

John hoped that Mudslinger could join the Top Hogs. But before he started training him, he wanted to give the young pig time to get used to his new life. There was one thing Mudslinger needed to learn right away, however. Even though John's pigs ate and slept inside the house, the bathroom was outside!

John's house had a special "hog door," so the pigs could let themselves out. All they had to do was push through the door whenever they needed to go to the bathroom or wanted to lounge on the porch. But to come back in, the pigs had to put their noses behind the handle on the door. Then they could pull it open, just like a "people" door, and squeeze in. John would need to teach Mudslinger how to do that—or so he thought.

When the other pigs went outside, Mudslinger followed them through the hog door. John went out, too, to see what Mudslinger would do. When a pig opened the door to go back in, Mudslinger watched closely. Then he walked up to the door, pulled it open with his nose, and strolled in. Mudslinger had taught himself!

It was clear that Mudslinger was a superfast learner. So John decided to start training him right away. "I didn't want to hold him back," he said.

John took Mudslinger into the living room. That's where he trained all his pigs. John started by giving the pig a treat—a bite of banana or apple, or a grape. Next, John said, "Good," and handed Mudslinger another treat. He did this over and over. Soon, Mudslinger learned that "good" meant a treat.

Smart as a Pig

Have you ever heard that pigs are smarter than dogs? While scientists don't know that for sure, they do know that pigs are extremely intelligent. Pigs learn very quickly, and often on the first try. In fact, studies show that pigs learn some tasks as quickly as chimpanzees. Pigs are also similar to humans. Like us, pigs are able to think through problems and find clever solutions. In one study, pigs were able to use mirrors to find food that had been hidden out of sight!

Now Mudslinger was ready to learn his first trick. John taught it to him one step at a time. First he held a stick up to Mudslinger. He wanted the pig to touch it with his nose. Sometimes it takes a little while for an animal to do what John wants. Not Mudslinger.

Did You Know?

Pigs don't see very well, but they have a sharp sense of smell. In some places they are used to sniff out rare mushrooms called truffles.

He figured it out right away. He pressed his snout to the stick. John said, "Good," and gave him a treat.

Next John tried to get Mudslinger to take a step to touch the stick. When he did, John said, "Good." He handed Mudslinger a grape. Treat by treat, he led the pig around in a circle.

The next step for Mudslinger was to learn to do something on cue. Right before John thought Mudslinger was going to sit, he said, "Sit." Then he rewarded him when he did it. Pretty soon Mudslinger knew what to do when John said, "Sit."

John had Mudslinger practice his tricks in different places. They practiced at different times of the day and in a different order. John needed to know that Mudslinger could do the tricks wherever the show went.

John trained Mudslinger six days a week, like an Olympic athlete. He knew that Mudslinger really wanted to learn. How did he know? Mudslinger told John by his behavior.

Mudslinger was always kind to the other pigs—unless one of them came into the living room during his training time. Then, SQUEAL! Mudslinger grunted and snorted and ran at the other pig. He chased him right out of the room! Mudslinger wanted to learn, and no pig was going to stop him.

Some people might call Mudslinger "pigheaded." Pigs have a reputation for being stubborn. But John thinks that they are just being cautious (sounds like CAW-shus).

Mudslinger was especially good at problem solving. One time, John tried to teach him how to push a golf ball into a ring on the ground. Mudslinger couldn't get the ball over the edge of the ring. But he knew what John wanted. So he picked up the ring and placed it around the ball!

Mudslinger wasn't in training all the time. Like the other potbellies on the ranch, he was a pet. John and Mudslinger cuddled. They touched noses. They slurped ice cream together almost every night.

One day John went looking for his sweatshirt. "Debbie, have you seen it?" he asked his wife. He searched all over the house. Finally, he checked the pigs' bedroom. Sure enough, Mudslinger had taken it. He had placed it on top of the pile of blankets. *Sweet dreams, little piggy.*

Mudslinger toots his own horn at a Top Hogs show. The little pig loves to perform.

Chapter 3

HIGH on the HOG

Mudslinger learned tricks faster than any other pig John had trained. After only two months, he was ready to be in the Top Hogs show.

At first, John had Mudslinger perform small tricks. But in no time, the pig was ready for harder tricks. In one trick, Mudslinger put his mouth up to a microphone. He pretended to be singing an Elvis song. The audience laughed. Then he raised an American flag with his snout. The audience applauded.

In another trick, John held up a hoop. He motioned for Mudslinger to jump through it. Mudslinger gave John a funny look. He seemed to say, *No way.* Then he stretched his neck. He took the hoop in his mouth and lowered it to the stage. He *walked* through!

Later in the act, Mudslinger hopped on a skateboard. Another pig pushed him across the stage. *Grind on, Tony Hawg!*

Has Mudslinger ever had stage fright? Only once. John always takes the animals on the stage before a performance. He wants them to feel comfortable when it's showtime. They look around. They walk across the stage. One time, Mudslinger walked onstage and froze. John was never sure what happened. He thinks Mudslinger saw a shadow and became afraid. So far it hasn't happened again.

Mudslinger was less than a year old when he was invited to be on TV. National Geographic was making a show called *Brilliant Beasts* that would tell stories about smart pigeons, dogs, and hogs. They had heard about the pig prodigy (sounds like PRAH-duh-gee) and wanted to feature him in an episode called *Hog Genius*.

Mudslinger never missed a cue. The filmmaker said that he had never seen a pig do everything it was asked to do. When it was time to film Mudslinger, he would joke, "Time for another slingshot!"

Kids Can Help

John Vincent adopted Mudslinger through the Pig Placement Network (PPN). PPN workers rescue unwanted or abandoned pet potbellied pigs. Then they help find them loving new homes. You can also help homeless pigs and other animals. Here are some ways:

- Volunteer to clean cages at shelters.
- Help collect food and supplies for shelters.
- Organize a penny drive. Set up jars or cans at school. Ask people to donate pennies. Send the money to an animal rescue group.

Always check with your parents first, and ask at the animal shelter about helping.

Soon after that, Mudslinger was invited to be on another TV show. This time it was an animal talent contest. John and Mudslinger trotted out onstage.

"Wave hello to everybody," said John. Mudslinger waved his foot.

"Now play dead." Mudslinger rolled onto his side.

John threw a toy. "Fetch this for me." Mudslinger brought it back. Then Mudslinger lifted the lid of a toy box with his nose. He dropped the toy in.

Finally, John set up a soccer goal. He put orange cones in a row. It was Mudslinger's hardest trick. "I want to see you move in and out," he told Mudslinger. Mudslinger pushed the soccer ball around each cone.

"I hope he has a nose for the goal," John said. Mudslinger gave the ball a shove. It hit the goalpost. "Aaawwww," said someone in the audience. But he didn't know Mudslinger. That pig didn't give up. He pushed the ball one more time. Goal!

Mudslinger won the talent contest. The host tried to put a medal on him. But Mudslinger wasn't interested. The host put it on John instead.

The little ham was becoming quite famous. In 2010, he took another step on his road to stardom. A major TV network was hosting an even bigger pet talent contest. Pet stars from all around the nation were invited to compete. Mudslinger was one of them.

The show's producers flew John and Mudslinger to New York City. They put them up in a fancy hotel. Did Mudslinger go hog wild and call for room service? No, but the little porker and John did enjoy their nightly ice cream.

The next day was the show. Mudslinger competed against four other talented animals. There was a bird that played golf and a dog that played cards. There was a water-skiing squirrel and a dog that jumped rope. But Mudslinger was a trouper. He did his tricks perfectly, just like always. And he won! But that was just the first round of the contest.

Did You Know?

Pigs have four toes on each foot. But they only walk on two, so they look like they are on their tiptoes.

A little while later, John and Mudslinger came back to New York to compete in the finals. While they were there, they visited the Pig Placement Network. The lady who had rescued Mudslinger was happy to see him doing so well.

Then John and Mudslinger went to the TV studio for the big event. Mudslinger beat all the other animals again! He was declared the most talented pet in America. He has the trophy (sounds like TRO-fee) to prove it!

These days Mudslinger and the other Top Hogs perform at schools, libraries,

Did You Know?

Piggy banks aren't named after pigs. They were named after pots made of special clay, called "pygg," that people kept extra money in.

county fairs, and rodeos all over the country. Mudslinger hardly ever makes a mistake onstage. But he can get carried away. John has an instrument he calls a "hogs-a-phone." It's a stand with bicycle horns of different sizes and sounds. The pigs play their own songs on it. When this musical performance is over, John moves the hogs-a-phone to the back of the stage. But sometimes Mudslinger isn't finished. He tiptoes to the back of the stage and makes more music!

Some research suggests that math and musical talent go together. That's true for Mudslinger. He now knows an amazing math trick. John sets up five cups. Each cup has a number from one to five painted on it. John lines them up in order by number. He asks Mudslinger, "What is one plus two?" He uses his fingers to help ask the question. Mudslinger walks along the cups, stops, and picks up the cup marked "3." He brings it to John.

Then John asks him, "Mudslinger, what's two plus three?" Mudslinger walks in front of the cups again. He looks at them carefully. He pauses by cup number three, but moves on. Finally, he picks up cup number five.

There's no doubt about it: Mudslinger is one brainy hog. John knew from day one that the little pig was hungry to learn. He still is. So what's next for Mudslinger? Algebra?

THE END

DON'T MISS!

NATIONAL GEOGRAPHIC KiDS **CHAPTERS**

HORSE ESCAPE ARTIST!

And More True Stories of **Animals Behaving Badly**

By Ashlee Brown Blewett

Turn the page for a sneak preview . . .

Mariska wears colorful reindeer antlers to celebrate her first Christmas at Misty Meadows Farm.

Chapter 1

A FAIRY-TALE HORSE

It was a sunny morning in Midland, Michigan, U.S.A. A cool breeze blew through an open kitchen window at the Bonem home on Misty Meadows Farm. Mrs. Sandy Bonem was getting ready to cook breakfast.

Suddenly, a big black shadow loomed past the window. Wait! Make that *three* big black shadows. Mrs. Bonem glanced out the window, and her heart sank to her toes.

"HON!" she yelled across the house to her husband, Don Bonem. "The horses are out! They're in the backyard!"

Mrs. Bonem dashed to the back door. Slowly, she slid open the door and stepped onto the deck. "Trienke (sounds like TREN-kuh)," Mrs. Bonem called softly. She inched down the stairs. She stepped onto a thick bed of green grass and stopped. She didn't want to startle the herd.

The horses' ears twitched. They lifted their heads and turned toward the voice. Their bodies tensed. They could easily flee.

"Trienke, *come*," Mrs. Bonem said.

For a split second nothing happened. Then, all three horses lunged. They sprinted toward Mrs. Bonem like a pack of playful puppies. They kissed her cheeks with their big wet horse lips.

"Oh you guys!" she said. She stroked their foreheads and exhaled a deep sigh of relief. "How did you get out here?" She turned toward the barn. "Let's go," she said. All three horses followed her.

Minutes later, Mrs. Bonem reached the large sliding barn door. It looked like a clever horse had nudged it open. Mrs. Bonem turned and eyed the herd. Trienke is a ten-year-old mare, or female. She's the mother of the other two horses, Mariska (sounds like Muh-RIS-kah) and Wietse (sounds like WEET-sah).

Trienke is the boss mare, or leader, of

Did You Know?

There are about 400 types, or breeds, of horses.

the herd. But Mrs. Bonem knew that Trienke didn't always call the shots. Instead, Mrs. Bonem fingered Mariska as the guilty one. Mariska had a long record of making mischief.

The Misty Meadows horses are a breed known as Friesian (sounds like FREE-shun). Friesian horses come from Friesland (sounds like FREES-land)—a region of the Netherlands, a country in Europe. Friesians have all-black, shiny coats. And they're strong.

Long ago, Friesian horses carried knights into battle. "They look like a fairy-tale horse," Mrs. Bonem says. That's what first made her fall in love with the breed.

When Mr. and Mrs. Bonem decided to buy their first horse, it was a Friesian, of course. But first they built a barn. And instead of building just one horse stall in it, they built ten. With the extra room, other people could pay the Bonems to keep their horses at Misty Meadows, too.

A short while later, a family that lived down the street asked the Bonems to keep their two quarter horses at Misty Meadows. And the Bonems bought Trienke, their first Friesian.

Trienke was five years old when the Bonems got her in 2003. The next spring she gave birth to Mariska. Now the Bonems had four horses to look after.

As a baby, Mariska was allowed out of her stall to roam the barn during the day. The young horse followed Mrs. Bonem everywhere.

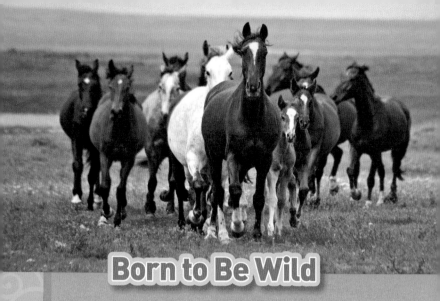

Born to Be Wild

Wild horses live in family groups called herds. Herd members form strong bonds, or ties. They nuzzle each other's faces and necks. Each herd member has a specific place, or rank, in the group. The same is true for pet horses. The horses higher up in rank protect those lower down the line. Horses like to be near other horses. This is true even if they're not related. Pet horses even treat humans like members of their herd.

Soon Mariska had Mrs. Bonem's heart wrapped around her tiny little hooves. Mariska's antics, or pranks, began when she was about six months old. Mrs. Bonem entered the horse's stall one morning. Mariska walked over. She nuzzled Mrs. Bonem's neck. Then she wrapped her teeth around the zipper tab on Mrs. Bonem's coat.

ZIP, ZIP! Mariska pulled the zipper up and down. Up and down. "You silly horse," Mrs. Bonem said.

Next, Mariska targeted hair ties. Whenever Mrs. Bonem bent down to clean her stall, Mariska lurked nearby. With one yank she would pull the fluffy red or blue hair tie off of Mrs. Bonem's ponytail. Then she'd try to eat it! *Chomp, chomp.*

Want to know what happens next? Be sure to check out *Horse Escape Artist!* Available wherever books and ebooks are sold.

INDEX

Boldface indicates illustrations.

MORE INFORMATION

To find more information about the animal species featured in this book, check out these articles and websites:

"Doggy daring takes Otis skydiving," the *Sacramento Bee* (newspaper article and video)
www.sacbee.com/2011/08/16/3840235/doggy-daring-takes-otis-skydiving.html

Knoxville Zoo website
www.knoxville-zoo.org/animals_attractions/animal_guide/birds/congo_african_grey_parrot.aspx

National Geographic "Animals: Domestic Dog"
animals.nationalgeographic.com/animals/mammals/domestic-dog

National Geographic "Animals: Parrot"
animals.nationalgeographic.com/animals/birds/parrot

National Geographic "Creature Features: Pigs"
kids.nationalgeographic.com/kids/animals/creaturefeature/pigs

Top Hogs: Family-Fun Performances website
www.tophogs.com

**This book is dedicated to
a superstar in my life, my Aunt Joan. —MRD**

CREDITS

Cover, 4–5, 6, Knoxville Zoo; 10 (UPRT), Andrew Walmsley/NPL/
Minden Pictures; 10 (LOLE), James Steidl/Shutterstock; 16,
Knoxville Zoo; 23, Mark Wilson/The Boston Globe via Getty Images;
26, Knoxville Zoo; 30 (UPLE), BlueParrot/Shutterstock; 30 (LORT),
Fedor Selivanov/Shutterstock; 36–37, Autumn Cruz/Sacramento
Bee/Zuma Press; 38, Danielle D. Hughson/Getty Images; 42 (UPLE),
Tsekhmister/Shutterstock; 42 (UPRT), Alexia Khruscheva/
Shutterstock; 48, Sacramento Bee/Zuma Press; 55, Bettmann/
Corbis; 58, Sacramento Bee/Zuma Press; 65, Eddy Joaquim/Getty
Images; 68–69, Debbie Vincent; 70, John Vincent; 75, Ja Ritnetikun/
Shutterstock; 80, Dan Larson; 85, John Vincent; 90, Dan Larson; 94
(UPLE), NOAHARC/iStockphoto; 101, Zuzule/Shutterstock; 102, cour-
tesy of Sandy and Don Bonem; 108, © Taiga/Dreamstime; 111,
Knoxville Zoo

ACKNOWLEDGMENTS

My heartfelt thanks to:

My editor, Marfé Ferguson Delano, who taught me so much about
strong verbs, strong story, and great writing; Will da Silva, skydiving companion of Otis, for his generosity in sharing Otis's story;
Tina Rolen, Teresa Collins, and Nikki Edwards at the Knoxville Zoo
in Tennessee for their expertise and help in introducing me to
Einstein's world (and a special thanks to Einstein for speaking to
me on the phone!); John Vincent, owner and trainer of Mudslinger,
for his extraordinary help; Paige Towler, for her pig sidebars; and
as always, my family for their help and support in every way.